FOSSIL RIDGE PUBLIC LIBRARY DISTRICT
W9-CCN-007

Ancient Orbiters

Ancient Orbiters

By Sue Whiting

NATIONAL GEOGRAPHIC

WASHINGTON D.C.

One of the world's largest nonprofit scientific and educational organizations, the National Geographic Society was founded in 1888 "for the increase and diffusion of geographic knowledge." Fulfilling this mission, the Society educates and inspires millions every day through its magazines, books, television programs, videos, maps and atlases, research grants, the National Geographic Bee, teacher workshops, and innovative classroom materials. The Society is supported through membership dues, charitable gifts, and income from the sale of its educational products. This support is vital to National Geographic's mission to increase global understanding and promote conservation of our planet through exploration, research, and education.

For more information, please call
1-800-NGS-LINE (647-5463) or write to the following address:
National Geographic Society
1145 17th Street N.W.
Washington, D.C. 20036-4688
U.S.A.

For information about special discounts for bulk purchases, please contact
National Geographic Books Special Sales at ngspecsales@ngs.org

Visit the Society's Web site: www.nationalgeographic.com

Text revised from *A Guide to the Planets* in the National Geographic Windows on Literacy program from National Geographic School Publishing, © 2004 National Geographic Society

Published by National Geographic Society.
Washington, D.C. 20036

Design by Project Design Company

Printed in the United States

Library of Congress Cataloging-in-Publication Data

Whiting, Sue.
Ancient orbiters : a guide to the planets / by Sue Whiting.
p. cm. -- (National Geographic science chapters)
Includes bibliographical references and index.
ISBN-13: 978-0-7922-5945-9 (lib. binding)
ISBN-10: 0-7922-5945-9 (lib. binding)
1. Planets. 2. Solar system. I. Title. II. Series.
QB601.W63 2006
523.4--dc22

2006016358

Photo Credits
Front Cover: © Antonio M Rosario/ Iconica/ Getty Images; Spine: © PhotoDisc/ Getty Images; Endpaper: © PhotoDisc/ Getty Images; 2-3: © Getty Images; 6: © PhotoDisc/ Getty Images; 7: © Gary Bell/ Ocean Images; 8: © Art Wolfe/ Getty Images; 10: © Antonio M Rosario/ Iconica/ Getty Images; 12-13: © National Geographic; 14: © Mark Garlick/ Science Photo Library; 16: © NASA/ Science Photo Library; 17, 18: © PhotoDisc/ Getty Images; 19: © NASA; 20: © US Geological Survey/ Science Photo Library; 21: © NASA; 22, 23: © PhotoDisc/ Getty Images; 24: © Getty Images; 25, 26-27: © PhotoDisc/ Getty Images; 28, 29: © Science Photo Library; 30: © PhotoDisc/ Getty Images; 31: © NASA/ Science Photo Library; 32: © NASA; 33: © NASA/ Science Photo Library; 34: © Lynette Cook/ Science Photo Library; 35: © NASA.

Contents

Earth is the only planet known to have living things.

Welcome to Planet Earth

Earth looks like a big blue marble from space. It looks blue because of our many oceans, rivers, and lakes. Our planet is sometimes called the "water planet" because most of its surface is covered with water. Without water, nothing could live on Earth.

Fish swim in Earth's many oceans.

Penguins walk across the ice in Antarctica.

Plants and animals can be found on all parts of Earth. Some animals and plants live underwater. Others live in frozen, icy places. Still others live in grasslands, forests, or deserts.

Earth is surrounded by air. The air that surrounds a planet is called its atmosphere. There are many different gases in Earth's atmosphere, including the oxygen we need

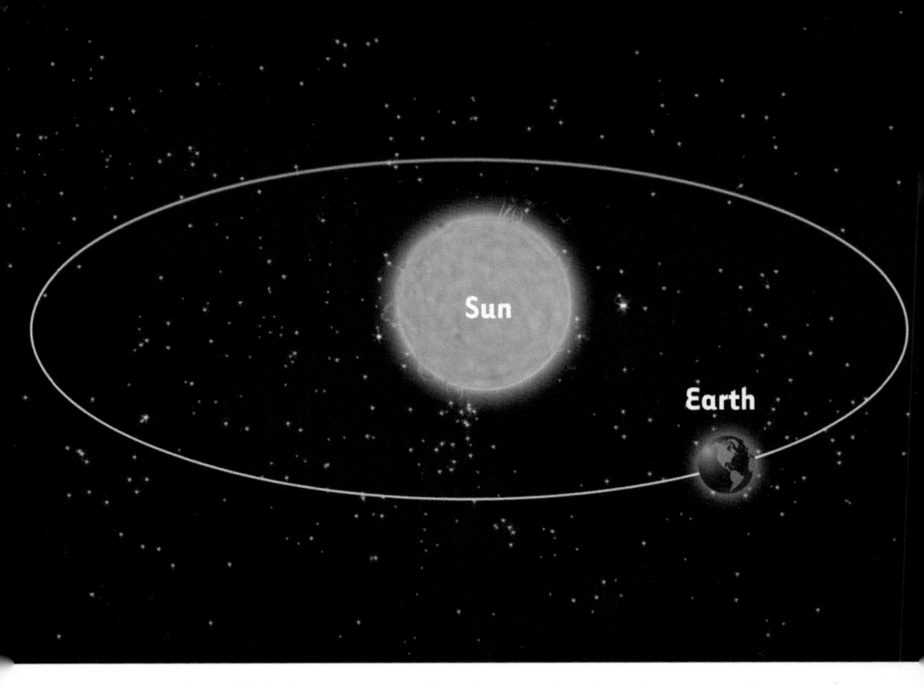

It takes 365 days, or one Earth year, for Earth to travel once around the sun.

to breathe. The atmosphere is like a blanket wrapped around the planet. It protects us from heat and cold.

Earth is the third planet from the sun. The sun is actually a star, or a giant ball of gas that sends out rays of heat and light. Earth moves in a circular path around the sun. The path a planet follows as it moves around the sun is called its orbit.

Light from the sun makes most life on Earth possible.

Chapter 1

The Solar System

Earth is not the only planet. In fact, it is just one of nine planets that orbit around the sun. The sun and the planets that orbit it are called the solar system.

Our solar system was formed about 4.5 billion years ago. In addition to the sun and nine planets, our solar system also includes more than 150 moons and millions of asteroids and comets.

The planets closest to the sun are Mercury, Venus, Earth, and Mars. They are small, rocky planets with hard surfaces. They are called the inner planets because they are the planets closest to the sun.

The five planets farthest from the sun—Jupiter, Saturn, Uranus, and Neptune—are called the outer planets. These planets are very different from the inner planets. Jupiter,

Saturn, Uranus, and Neptune are huge planets made of gases. These planets do not have a solid surface. Pluto is the planet farthest from the sun. It is small and icy.

This painting shows the nine planets in our solar system. It does not show each planet's distance from the sun.

Living things can't survive the temperature extremes on Mercury.

Chapter 2

The Inner Planets

Mercury

Mercury is much smaller than Earth. It is about the same size as our moon. Mercury looks a lot like our moon, too. It is dotted with large round holes called craters that formed when meteoroids hit the planet.

Mercury is the planet closest to the sun. Unlike Earth, Mercury has very few gases surrounding it. Because Mercury has little or no atmosphere, the temperatures on Mercury are extreme. During the day, the temperature on Mercury soars to 800°F (427°C). At night, the temperature on

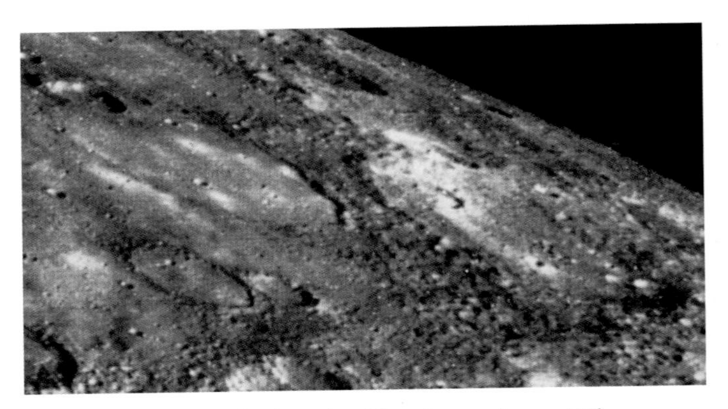

Mercury's surface looks a lot like the surface of the moon.

Mercury drops to –279°F (-173°C). Without an atmosphere, Mercury loses its heat as soon as it turns away from the sun.

Venus

Venus is Earth's closest neighbor. From Earth, Venus looks like a very bright star. It is almost the same size as Earth and was once thought of as Earth's twin. We now know that Venus is very different from Earth.

Venus is the hottest planet in our solar system. The temperature there is more than 842°F (450°C). Venus is surrounded by

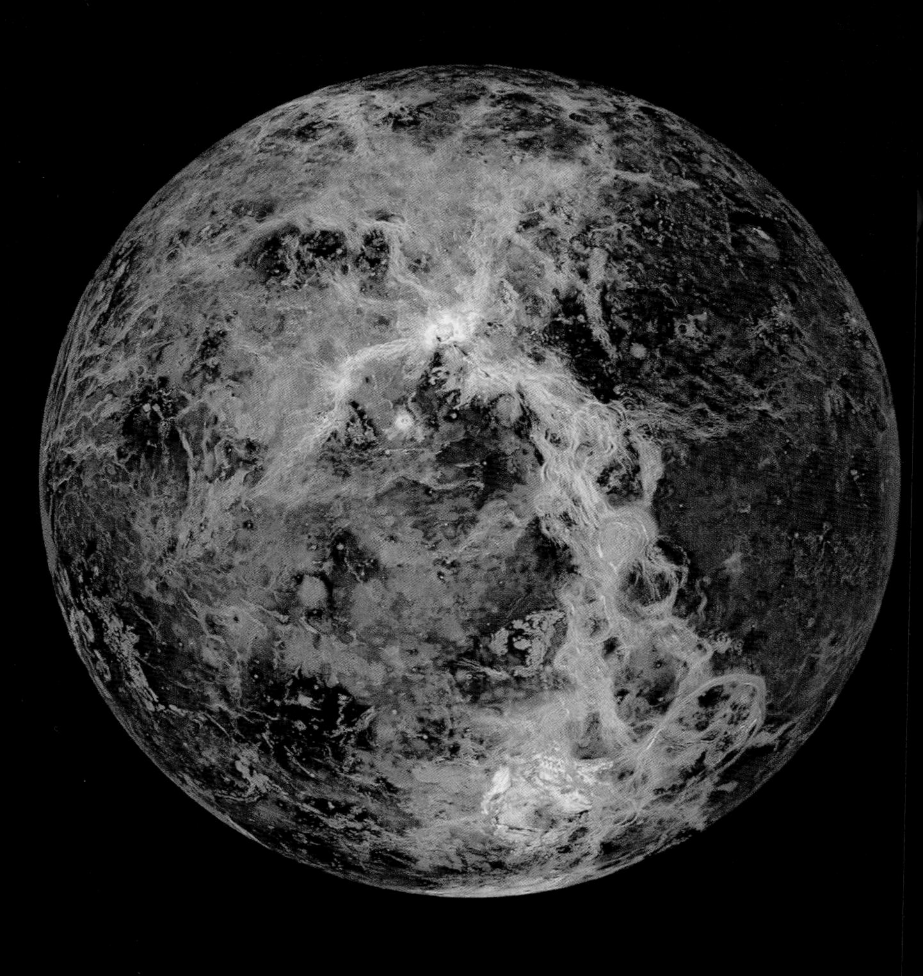

Venus is the easiest planet to spot in the night sky because its clouds reflect so much light.

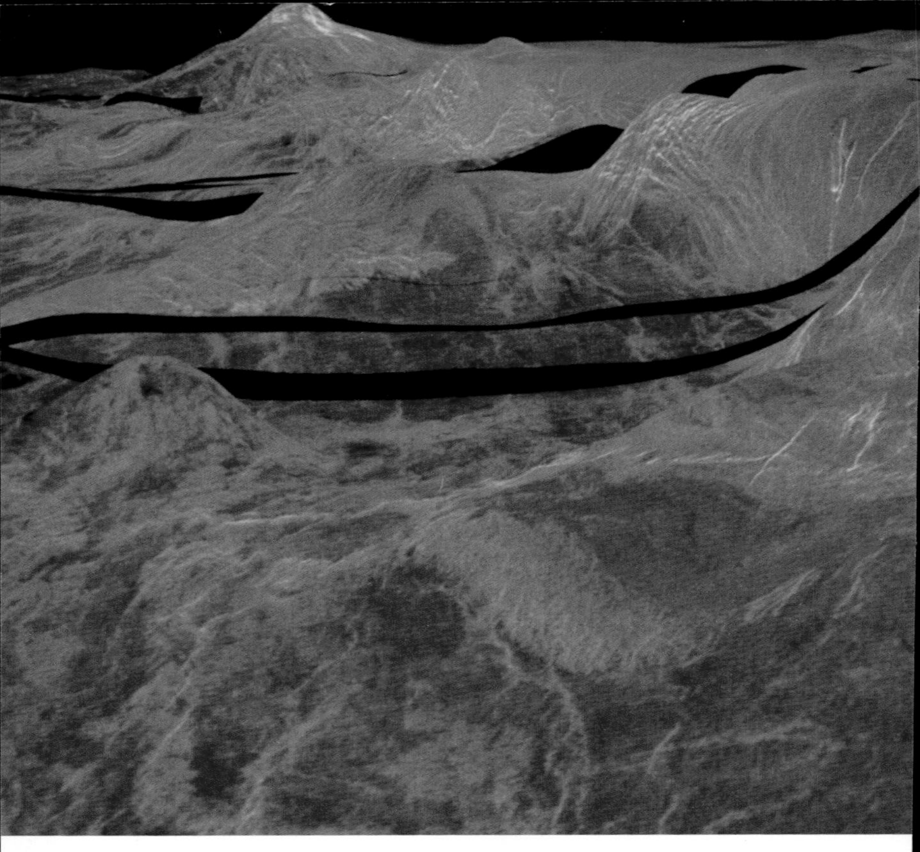

There are thousands of volcanoes on Venus.

thick, orange clouds. These clouds trap the sun's heat in much the same way as a glass windshield traps the sun's heat inside a car. There is no water on Venus. Scientists think that it would be impossible for life to exist on this planet.

Mars

Mars is the fourth planet from the sun. It is much smaller than Earth. It is also much colder. There is no liquid water on the surface of Mars so the ground is very dry. It looks like a red, rocky desert. The sky on Mars is pink! This is because Mars has many dust storms that send the red sand and dust from the surface into the atmosphere.

The wind on Mars creates sand dunes.

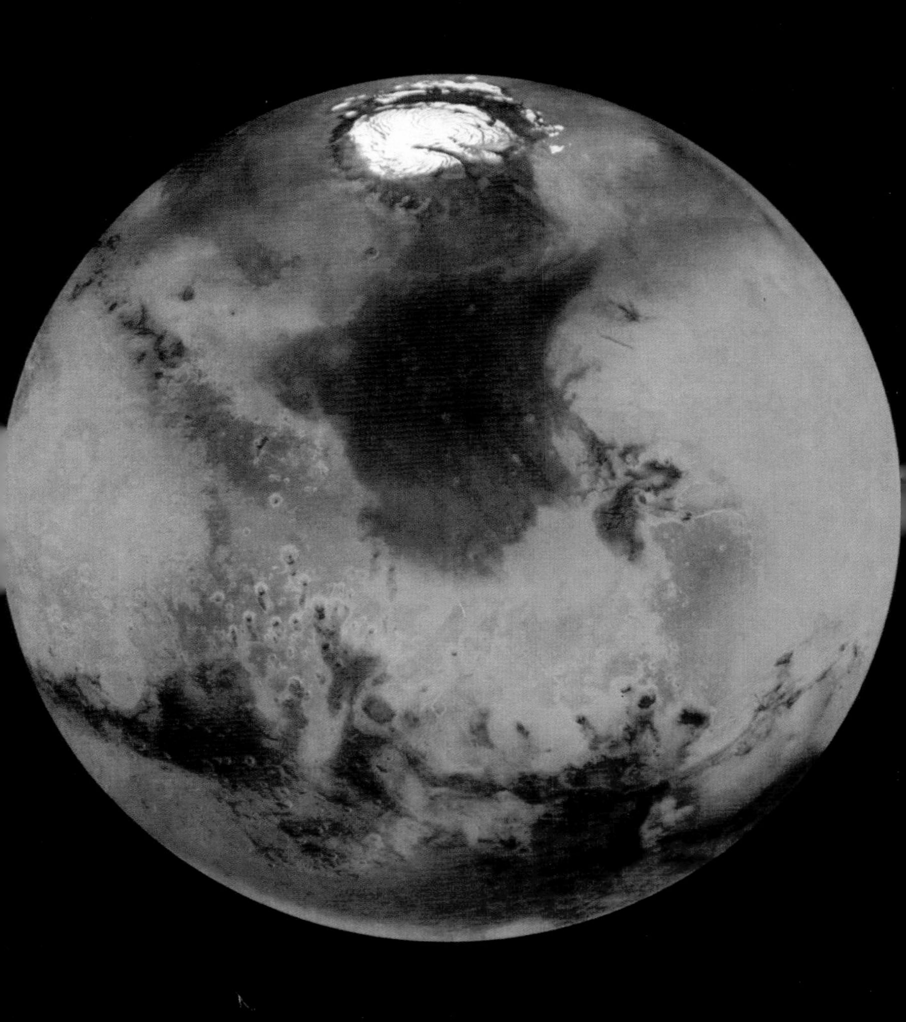

Despite its desert-like landscape, ice caps exist at both the North and South Poles on Mars.

Scientists sent space probes called rovers to Mars. The rovers collected images and data about the planet. The information they gathered showed that there was once water on Mars. Finding evidence of water on Mars makes scientists wonder if there was life on this planet at one time.

This model shows what a rover looked like as it explored Mars.

Jupiter is the fifth planet from the sun.

Chapter 3

The Outer Planets

Jupiter

Jupiter is huge. It is the largest planet in the solar system. Jupiter is so large that you could fit 1,300 Earths inside it. Unlike Earth, Jupiter does not have any solid ground. The planet is made of gases and is surrounded by storm clouds.

The colors in Jupiter's red spot are caused by chemicals in the atmosphere.

Jupiter appears very colorful when you look at it through a telescope. The planet has a large red spot on it that is more than three times wider than Earth. Scientists think this red spot is a fierce storm that has lasted for hundreds of years.

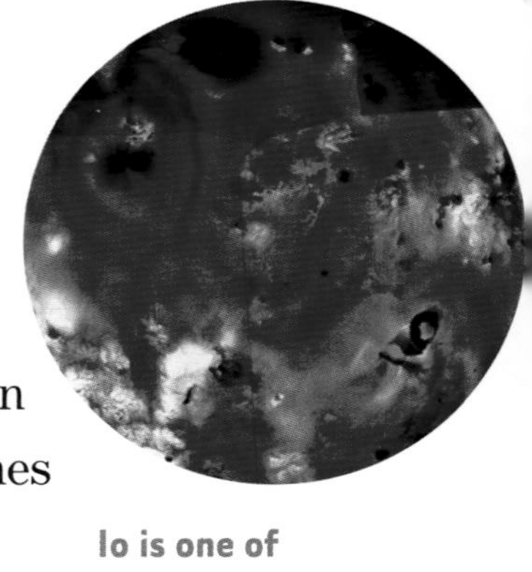

Io is one of Jupiter's moons.

At least 63 moons orbit Jupiter, and each of them is different. Some of the moons are covered in ice. The moon called Io is the most volcanic place in the entire solar system. One of Jupiter's moons is larger than the planets Mercury and Pluto.

Saturn

If you looked at Saturn through a telescope, you would see a colorful ball surrounded by beautiful rings. These rings are made of ice and rock. Some of the pieces of rock and ice inside Saturn's rings are as big as large houses.

Known for its beautiful rings, this enhanced color photograph also shows the bands of clouds that circle Saturn.

Saturn is the second largest planet in the solar system. Like Jupiter, Saturn is made of gases. Saturn is stormy like Jupiter, too. At least 47 moons orbit this gas giant. Scientists

There are more than a thousand rings around Saturn.

have recorded winds of about 1,000 miles per hour (1,609 km/h) on Saturn. These winds are more than four times stronger than the worst winds on Earth.

Uranus

Uranus is another giant gas planet that doesn't have a solid surface. Uranus isn't as big as Saturn and Jupiter, but it is still many times larger than Earth. It has at least 27 moons. When you look at Uranus through a telescope, it has a blue-green color. The gases that make up Uranus give it its color.

Uranus is often called the sideways planet because it spins on its side. Scientists believe that this may have happened when a meteoroid crashed into the planet. A meteoroid is a piece of rock and ice that travels through space.

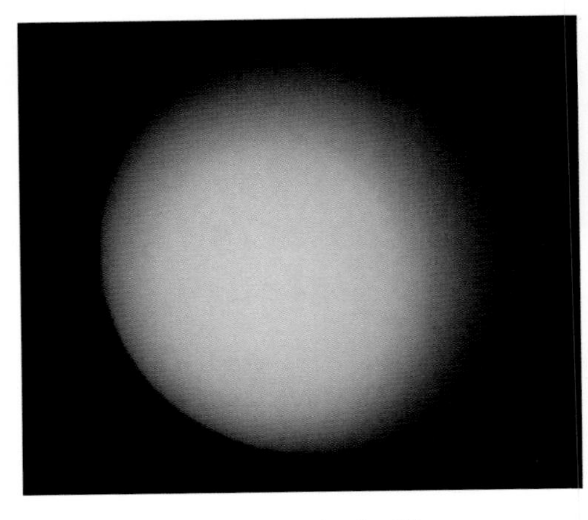

▲ Uranus sometimes looks like a dim star in the night sky.

Bands of rings surround Uranus.

You can't see Neptune from Earth without a telescope.

Neptune

Neptune looks like a smaller Uranus. The gases that make up Neptune also make it look blue. Like the other gas planets, Neptune is a stormy planet with fierce winds. Neptune even has a dark spot like Jupiter's red spot. Scientists call this spot the Great Dark Spot. It is a huge, long-lasting storm.

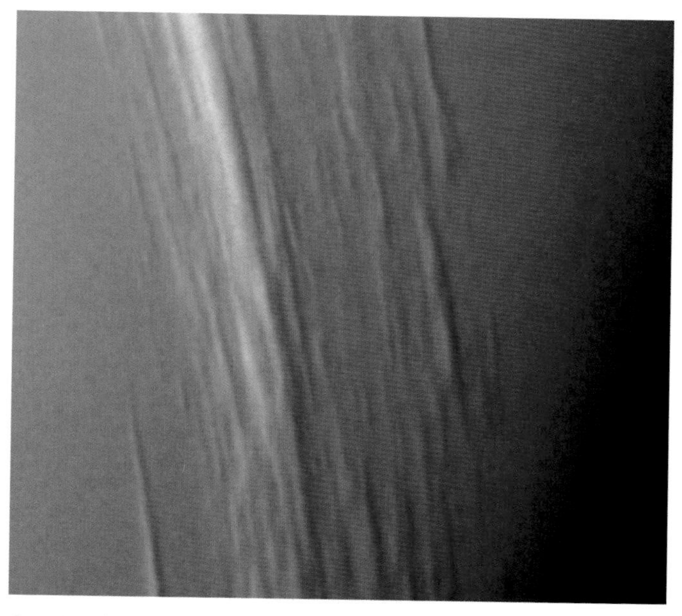

A striped pattern of clouds surrounds Neptune.

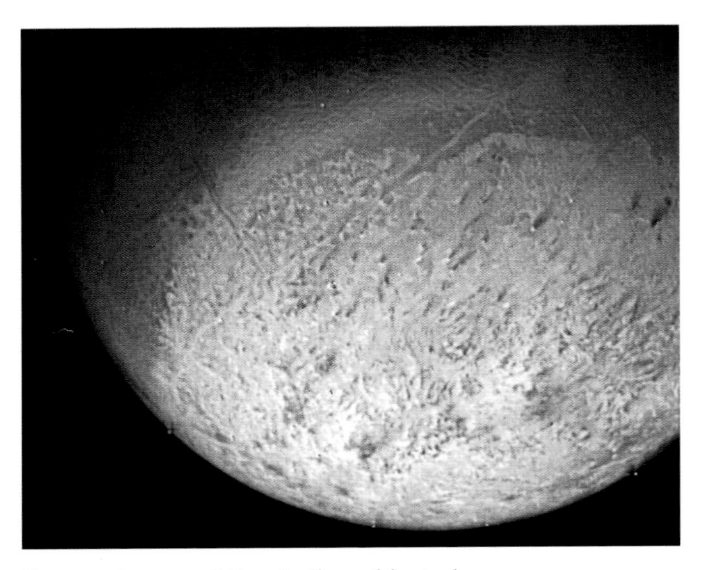

Neptune's moon Triton is the coldest place in the solar system.

At least 13 moons orbit Neptune. Neptune's largest moon is named Triton. It orbits Neptune in the opposite direction of the other moons.

It takes Neptune 165 Earth years to orbit the sun. Like Earth, Neptune has seasons. However, because it takes so long for Neptune to go around the sun, each season on Neptune lasts 41 Earth years!

Pluto

Pluto is the smallest planet in the solar system. It is very different from the huge gas planets that are closest to it. Pluto is a tiny, icy planet smaller than our moon. Its moon Charon is about half its size.

Pluto orbits the the sun in a part of the solar system known as the Kuiper Belt.

This photo of Pluto and its moon, Charon, was taken by the Hubble Space Telescope.

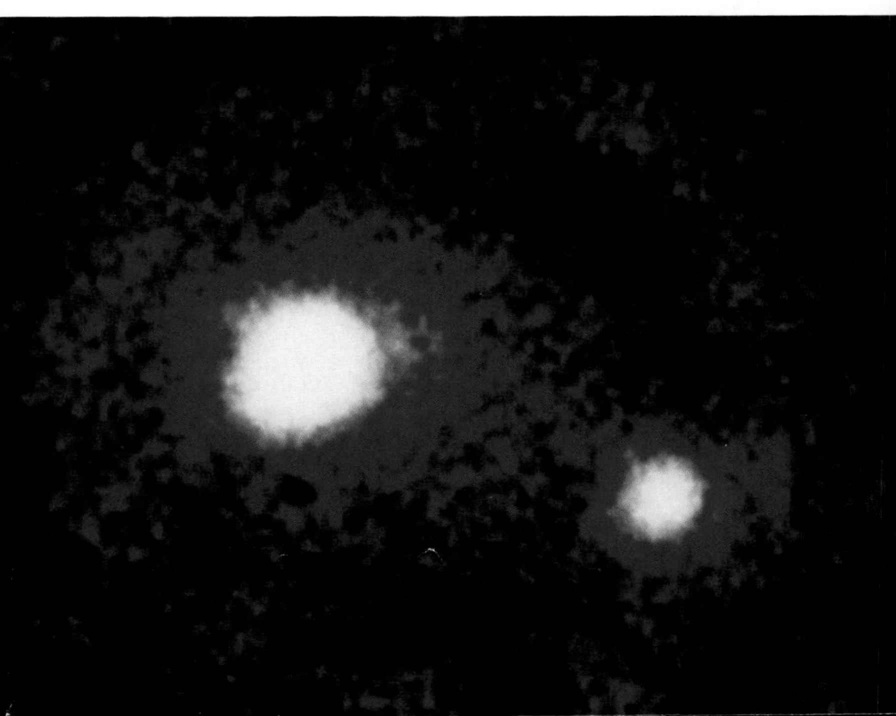

This painting shows what Pluto might look like. We don't know for sure because we know so little about the planet.

Here, at the outer edge of our solar system, thousands of large, icy objects orbit the the sun.

Because Pluto is so far away, we know little about it. In 2006 scientists launched a space probe designed to explore Pluto and the Kuiper Belt. The probe is expected to reach Pluto in 2015.

This painting shows the spacecraft that is on its way to Pluto.

How to Write an A+ Report

1. Choose a topic.

- Find something that interests you.
- Make sure it is not too big or too small.

2. Find sources.

- Ask your librarian for help.
- Use many different sources: books, magazine articles, and websites.

3. Gather information.

- Take notes. Write down the big ideas and interesting details.
- Use your own words.

4. Organize information.

- Sort your notes into groups that make sense.

- Make an outline. Put your groups of notes in the order you want to write your report.

5. Write your report.

- Write an introduction that tells what the report is about.
- Use your outline and notes as you write to make sure you say everything you want to say in the order you want to say it.
- Write an ending that tells about your report.
- Write a title.

6. Revise and edit your report.

- Read your report to make sure it makes sense.
- Read it again to check spelling, punctuation, and grammar.

7. Hand in your report!

Glossary

asteroid	a small rocky body that orbits the sun
atmosphere	the air that surrounds a planet
crater	a large hole in the ground that is shaped like a bowl
inner planets	the four planets that are closest to the sun
Kuiper Belt	a band of icy objects that orbit the sun at the outer edge of our solar system
meteoroid	a piece of rock in space
orbit	the path a planet follows as it moves around the sun
outer planets	the five planets that are farthest from the sun
oxygen	the gas all living things need to survive
solar system	a sun and the planets that orbit around it
star	a giant ball of gas that sends out rays of heat and light
telescope	a tool scientists use to look at planets and other objects in space

Further Reading

• Books •

Dyson, Marianne J. *Home on the Moon: Living on a Space Frontier.* Washington, DC: National Geographic Society, 2003. Ages 9-12, 64 pages.

Gifford, Clive. *The Kingfisher Facts and Records Book of Space.* New York, NY: Kingfisher, 2001. Ages 9-12, 64 pages.

Mitton, Jacqueline and Simon. *Scholastic Encyclopedia of Space.* New York, NY: Scholastic, 1998. Ages 9-12, 80 pages.

Ride, Sally and Tam O'Shaughnessy. *Exploring Our Solar System.* New York, NY: Crown Books for Young Readers, 2003. Ages 9-12, 112 pages.

Simon, Seymour. *Our Solar System.* New York, NY: Harper Collins, 1992. Ages 9-12, 64 pages.

Skurzynski, Gloria. *Discovering Mars.* Washington, DC: National Geographic Society, 1998. Ages 9-12, 48 pages.

Stars and Planets (First Pocket Guide Series). Washington, DC: National Geographic Society, 2002. Ages 8-10, 80 pages.

• Websites •

AeroSpaceGuide
http://www.aerospaceguide.net/space_kids.html

Astronomy for Kids
http://www.dustbunny.com/afk/planets/

Enchanted Learning
http://www.enchantedlearning.com/subjects/astronomy/

Kids Astronomy
http://www.kidsastronomy.com/solar_system.htm

National Aeronautics and Space Administration
http://education.nasa.gov/home/index.html

Science Monster
http://www.sciencemonster.com/planets.html

Wikipedia Online Encyclopedia
http://en.wikipedia.org/wiki/Planets

Index

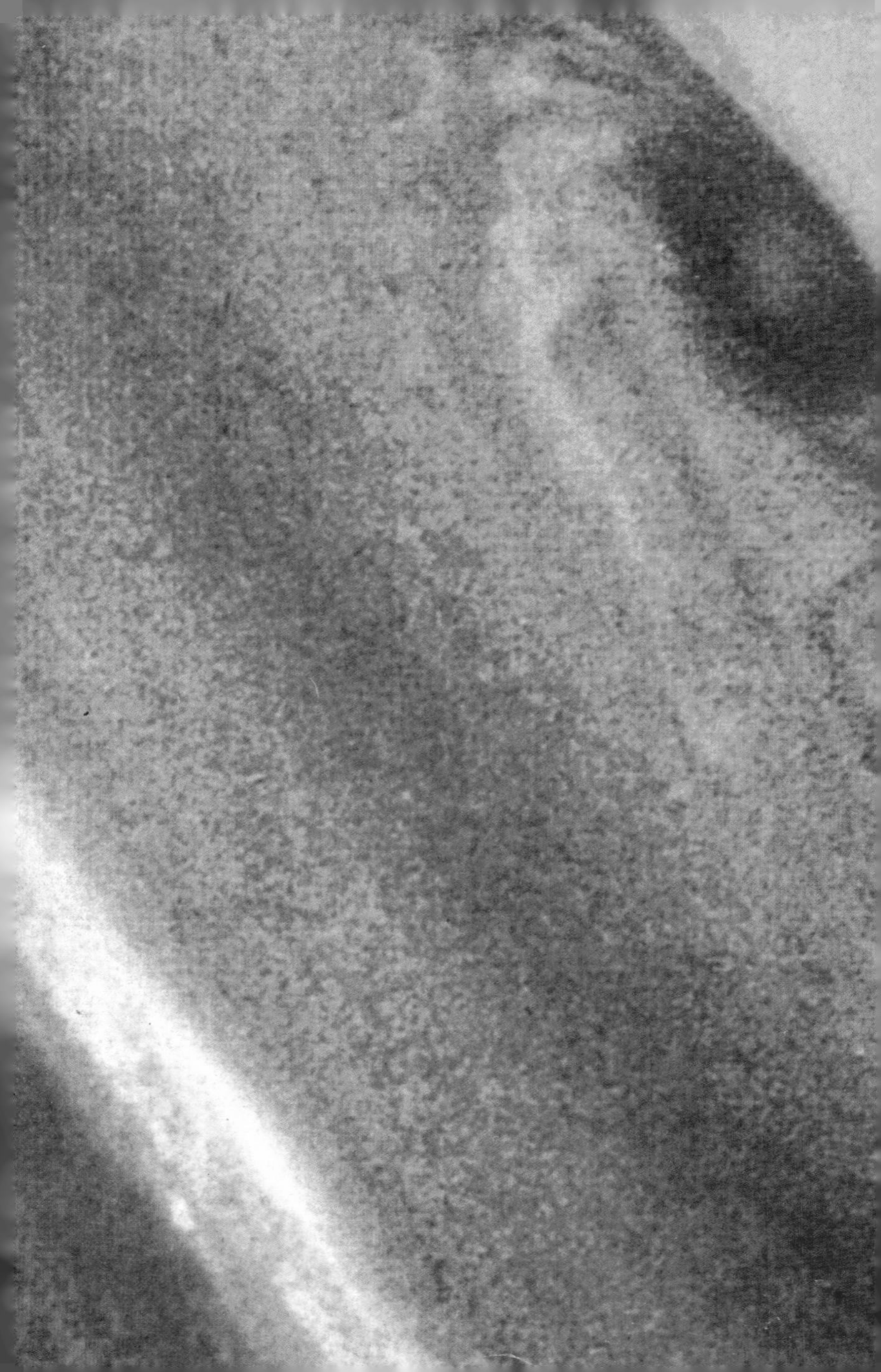